NERD SEARCH

STAR TREK™ THE NEXT GENERATION

BLOOPERS OF THE BORG

Written by **Glenn Dakin**

Art by **John Ross**

Colors by **Alan Craddock**

Consultant **Ben Robinson**

Eaglemoss. 2021
Premier Place, 2 & A Half Devonshire Square, London, EC2M 4UJ, UK
144, avenue Charles-de-Gaulle, 92200 Neuilly-sur-Seine, France

W*hat is a* Nerd Search? It is a puzzle book but not as you know it. We are giving you the chance to enjoy *STAR TREK: THE NEXT GENERATION* all over again—by ruining it with mistakes! We all love finding errors in our favorite shows, and we have added to the fun by inserting errors of a quirky kind.

This is not a simple 21st-century search-and-find book, it is more of a 24th-century, next-level challenge, with goofs in it that only a true *TREK* fan can spot! And along the way, we'll be saving the universe too.

And before we go any further, it's important to say that the whole book is one big continuity error, as none of the scenes, as we have depicted them, ever happened. Well, not quite like this. We have taken classic scenes and loaded them with extra action and hidden guest-stars for you to find … and prove you are the greatest *STAR TREK* nerd ever.

HOW TO USE THIS BOOK

TYPES OF PUZZLE

There are four types of puzzle in this book. They are contained in eight spreads based on classic episodes of *STAR TREK: THE NEXT GENERATION.*

1. CATCH THE CUBE

Spot the Borg Chaos Cube before it does too much damage!

2. NERD ALERT

Each spread has five continuity errors. It could be something subtle like a character in the wrong scene or the wrong costume. Or it could be an obvious blunder like a crew member from the wrong series, or a big name from a movie appearing! It might just be something that didn't happen, or something that would *never* happen in *TREK*.

3. THE ARTIFACT ANOMALY

Every scene contains 10 elements—characters, gadgets, weapons or some other item, from other episodes of the series. They are all themed to make them easier. In "The Big Goodbye" for example, all elements are from holodeck-related stories.

4. SUPER QUIBBLES

A special talking point that only true fans would know about. Maybe an item that was only mentioned in dialogue that never actually appeared on the screen. Or it could involve behind-the-scenes knowledge. Hard-core fans will know it when they see it!

THE SCORING SYSTEM

Use your scorecard to keep track of your progress

Answers ***on page 24***

CATCH THE CUBE: 10 points each.

NERD ALERT: 4 points each.

ARTIFACT ANOMALY: 2 points for spotting the out-of-context element and **3 points** for naming the episode it comes from, so a maximum of **5** for each.

At this stage you can score a possible 80 points per spread.

BUT WAIT! We have set our **Super Quibbles** at an incredible **215.5 points** each. This brings your possible top score across the whole book to the magic number of **2364**—the year that the adventures of Jean-Luc Picard and his crew started.

WE HAVE ENGAGED THE BORG ...

We love to rave on about our favorite TV shows and movies. But there is one thing we secretly enjoy more ... picking them apart. In an affectionate spirit, of course. And never in the history of TV has any phenomenon been dissected, and generally nerded over, as this one.

NEW KIND OF FAN

STAR TREK didn't just create a whole new style of TV, it also created a whole new kind of fan. *STAR TREK* fans didn't just want autographed photos of their heroes, they wanted to feel part of the show, explore its ideas, wear its costumes, speak its language. More than anything, when it ended in 1969, they wanted it back.

BRAVE GAMBLE

Endless letter-writing campaigns, conventions and lobbying helped to keep the dream alive. The original cast returned in movies, starting with *STAR TREK: THE MOTION PICTURE* in 1979. That wasn't quite the dream. The fans wanted it back as part of their everyday lives. And in 1987 it happened—but there was a catch. The original cast had become expensive, and maybe less inclined to the treadmill of a weekly TV show. Gene Roddenberry, the creator of the series, took a brave gamble in giving fans not their old show back, but a whole new vision.

STAR TREK: THE NEXT GENERATION was another case of making an inspired leap. Shows had been revived before, but not in a whole new guise, with fresh characters, set decades after the original. This was unheard of. It ignored the appeal of the original cast and depended entirely on the strength of the show's concept, its style, in fact—its culture.

UNCHARTED

This was uncharted territory … and boy, were the fans ready to get nerdy over of it! Anxieties abounded about the multiple changes and new ideas. Would it "feel" like *STAR TREK* without Kirk and Spock? Would it have the same internal consistency as the original? Would it be made with the same love?

UNEXPLORED

And then, on September 28th, 1987, our screens were filled by an immense, new—yet familiar—starship. Nostalgic string music evoked old memories of adventure. Then a figure with a clear-eyed, intense gaze stepped out of the shadows, and a voice of quiet authority said: "Captain's log, stardate 41153.7. Our destination is planet Deneb Four, beyond which lies the great unexplored mass of the Galaxy …" and we were hooked once again.

GREAT BIRD OF THE GALAXY

Expert fans had been waiting to catch the new series out. But by setting it in a further future, Roddenberry, "the Great Bird of the Galaxy," had already outmanoeuvred them. All the special effects were subtly different, because time had moved on, technology had changed. There was now a whole new rule book to be written.

SPACE JELLYFISH

Nevertheless, there were some blunders. Why in the very first story, did the tentacles of the giant space jellyfish act like they were under Earth gravity, when they were floating in space? In the second story, "The Naked Now," why (of all things!) when a screen showed the original series *Enterprise* did it show the wrong one—the redesigned movie version, not the actual ship that had been on the five-year mission? That blunder was considered serious enough

to be later digitally fixed. In "Yesterday's Enterprise" a temporal rift saw the crew fighting a war in a dark alternate timeline. At the end of the episode, when time had been 'fixed,' Geordi was still seen wearing the uniform from events that now never happened.

BEST-KNOWN BLUNDERS

In the show's big finale "All Good Things" the whole plot revolved around three *Enterprises*, in three different eras, combining to prevent a time-related disaster. Except one of the ships wasn't the *Enterprise* at all, it had been established in the first part of the story that it was the U.S.S. *Pasteur*—under Dr. Beverly Picard's command.

Perhaps the best-known blunder was a view of the Earth from the movie *STAR TREK: FIRST CONTACT*. It showed the planet from space—you could clearly see Australia, but there was no New Zealand! Fans—especially the Kiwis—howled. Did it not exist in the future?

NEW AUDIENCE

Regardless of the occasional blunder, *STAR TREK: THE NEXT GENERATION* was not only accepted by fans; it also won over a whole new audience and went on to exceed the success of the original by running to seven series.

BORG CHAOS

The series didn't really have that many blunders. So we have had to invent our own. In fact, with the help of the Borg we have brought chaos and confusion to the history of a great show. If order is to return to the world of Picard and his crew, it is up to you to *make it so* …

STAR TREK™

THE NEXT GENERATION

BLOOPERS OF THE BORG

IN THE 24TH CENTURY, THE STARSHIP ENTERPRISE-*D*, under the command of Captain Jean-Luc Picard, pursues its ongoing mission to seek out new life. This brings them into contact with the Borg, a cyborg race with the one aim of assimilating all other life into their collective.

Despite their incredible technology, the Borg find themselves repeatedly frustrated by Picard and his crew. Finally, in an attempt to defeat them, the Borg send eight Chaos Cubes back in time. They are targeted at key moments in the *Enterprise*'s adventures to disrupt its mission and destroy its legacy. You must help Picard and crew hunt down the cubes to prevent temporal disaster.

At the same time, to prove you are the greatest *STAR TREK: THE NEXT GENERATION* fan ever, tackle the puzzles on every page and keep a tally of your score.

Let's see what's out there ...

The Big Goodbye

Captain Picard is enjoying some recreation time as private eye Dixon Hill on the holodeck, when a power surge causes safety protocols to switch off. Now he and his crew really are facing the gangster Cyrus Redblock—with their lives at stake. Are their gooses cooked? **And will they be able to put the Borg Chaos Cube on ice?**

THE ARTIFACT ANOMALY

Hidden in every scene in this book are 10 ARTIFACTS—characters or elements of any kind from other episodes connected to a similar theme. The theme here is holodeck. **Can you find 10 holo-intrusions and name the episodes? Don't worry, *our* safety protocols are switched on.**

NERD ALERT

There are FIVE CALAMITOUS CONTINUITY ERRORS in this picture! There could be something happening out of sequence, a character in the wrong scene, or someone from completely the wrong series! **Find them now and keep your nose clean, pal …**

SUPER QUIBBLE
Can you spot the special talking point?

The Defector

The *Enterprise* has been lured into the Neutral Zone by the wily Romulans, who tricked a defector into giving Captain Picard a phoney story about a secret base. Luckily, even wilier old Picard prepared some Klingon back-up! **While retreating, don't forget to scan for the Borg Chaos Cube!**

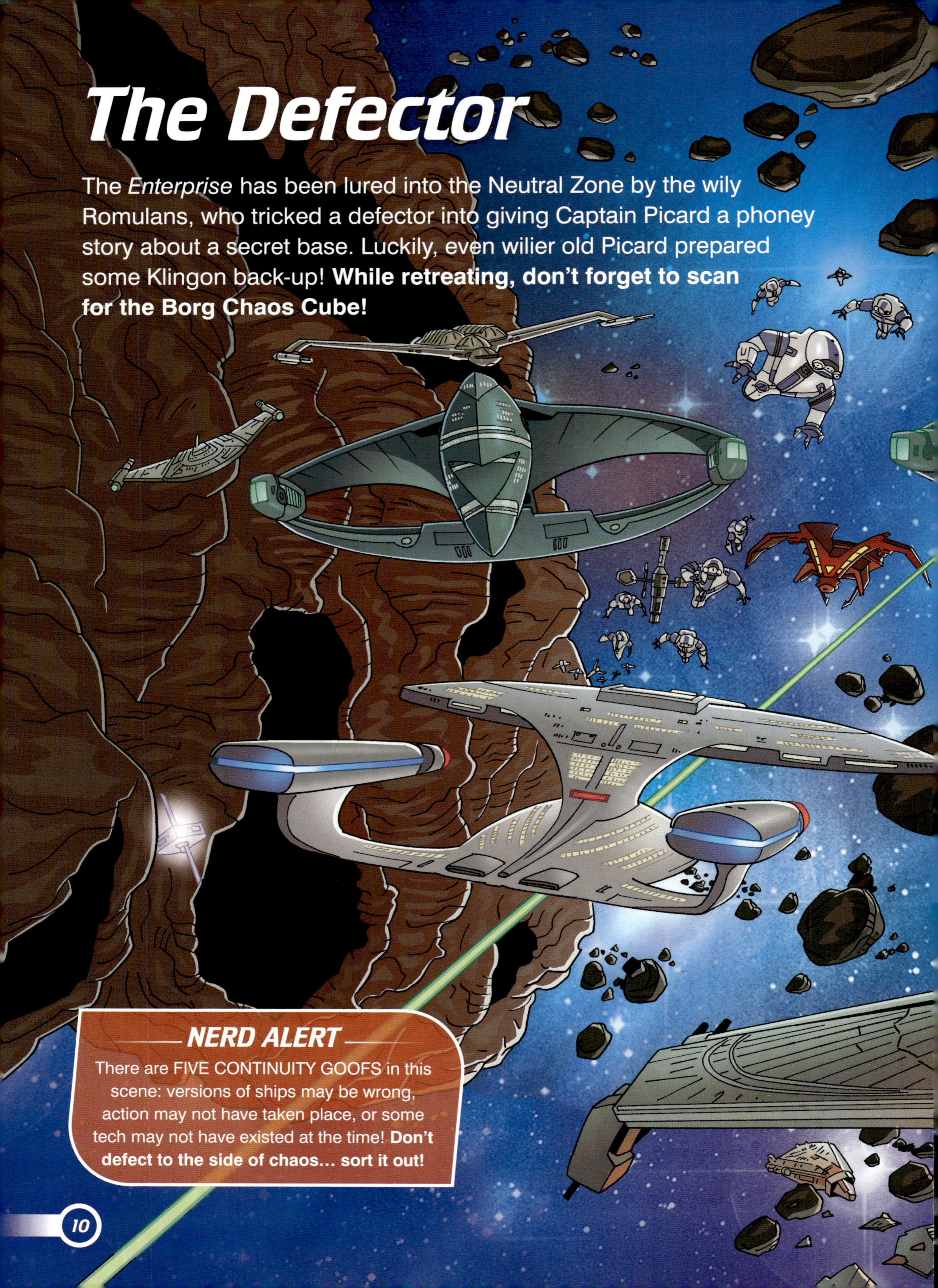

NERD ALERT

There are FIVE CONTINUITY GOOFS in this scene: versions of ships may be wrong, action may not have taken place, or some tech may not have existed at the time! **Don't defect to the side of chaos… sort it out!**

SUPER QUIBBLE
Can you spot the special talking point?

THE ARTIFACT ANOMALY

There are 10 ITEMS making a dangerous incursion into this scene and altering reality as we know it. They are all on the theme of space—its battles, dangers, and mysteries! **Power up your disruptors and target the intruders.**

Sarek

The *Enterprise* is taking the Federation Ambassador, Sarek, to a vital negotiation. Unfortunately, the usually calm Vulcan is being affected by a rare condition that makes him lose control of his feelings ... and transmit them to others! The logical outcome is chaos.
Can you keep control and find the Borg Chaos Cube as well?

SUPER QUIBBLE
Can you spot the special talking point?

THE ARTIFACT ANOMALY
Throughout this scene there are 10 ITEMS, characters, or props connected with other episodes containing ambassadors, emissaries, and representatives.
Can you spot them and name the episodes they come from?
NERD ALERT
There are FIVE CONTINUITY ERRORS in this scene. They could be characters in the wrong place at the wrong time or doing something that never really happened.
You should not need a mind meld with Sarek to detect them.

The Best of Both Worlds

Prepare to be assimilated! Captain Picard has been abducted by the Borg and is being held in a cube that is heading towards Earth! The *Enterprise* crew have launched a rescue mission. Will they be able to find the hidden cube as well? **In this case, resistance is not futile, it's vital… to save the day!**

SUPER QUIBBLE
Can you spot the special talking point?

THE ARTIFACT ANOMALY

In this scene are 10 ITEMS from other Borg, robot, or artificial sentience-themed episodes. Do your feeble human senses have the power to spot them? **Act fast or spend the rest of your life servicing your cyborg masters!**

NERD ALERT

Your life, as it has been, is over … unless you can spot the FIVE CONTINUITY ERRORS created by the evil Borg Chaos Cube. **They could be costume mistakes, characters in the wrong story, or just someone acting way out of character!**

Qpid

THE ARTIFACT ANOMALY

In affairs of the heart, three's a crowd, but there are 10 INTRUSIVE ELEMENTS trying to spoil Jean-Luc's romantic rescue of Vash. **They are all from Q-related episodes, or those with similar all-powerful nuisances—err… beings.**

Verily, the extra-dimensional being Q has transported Jean-Luc into a Robin Hood scenario in mediaeval England, for a lesson in love. Picard's old flame Vash is there, as Maid Marian. Naturally, Q is the Sheriff of Nottingham. But your personal duel must be with the Borg Chaos Cube. **Find it, so love can conquer all…**

SUPER QUIBBLE
Can you spot the special talking point?

NERD ALERT

You will not be a merry man (or woman) until you have spotted the FIVE CONTINUITY ERRORS in this swashbuckling scene. They may be details that are out of sequence or massive costume blunders.
Find them quick, mon Capitan!

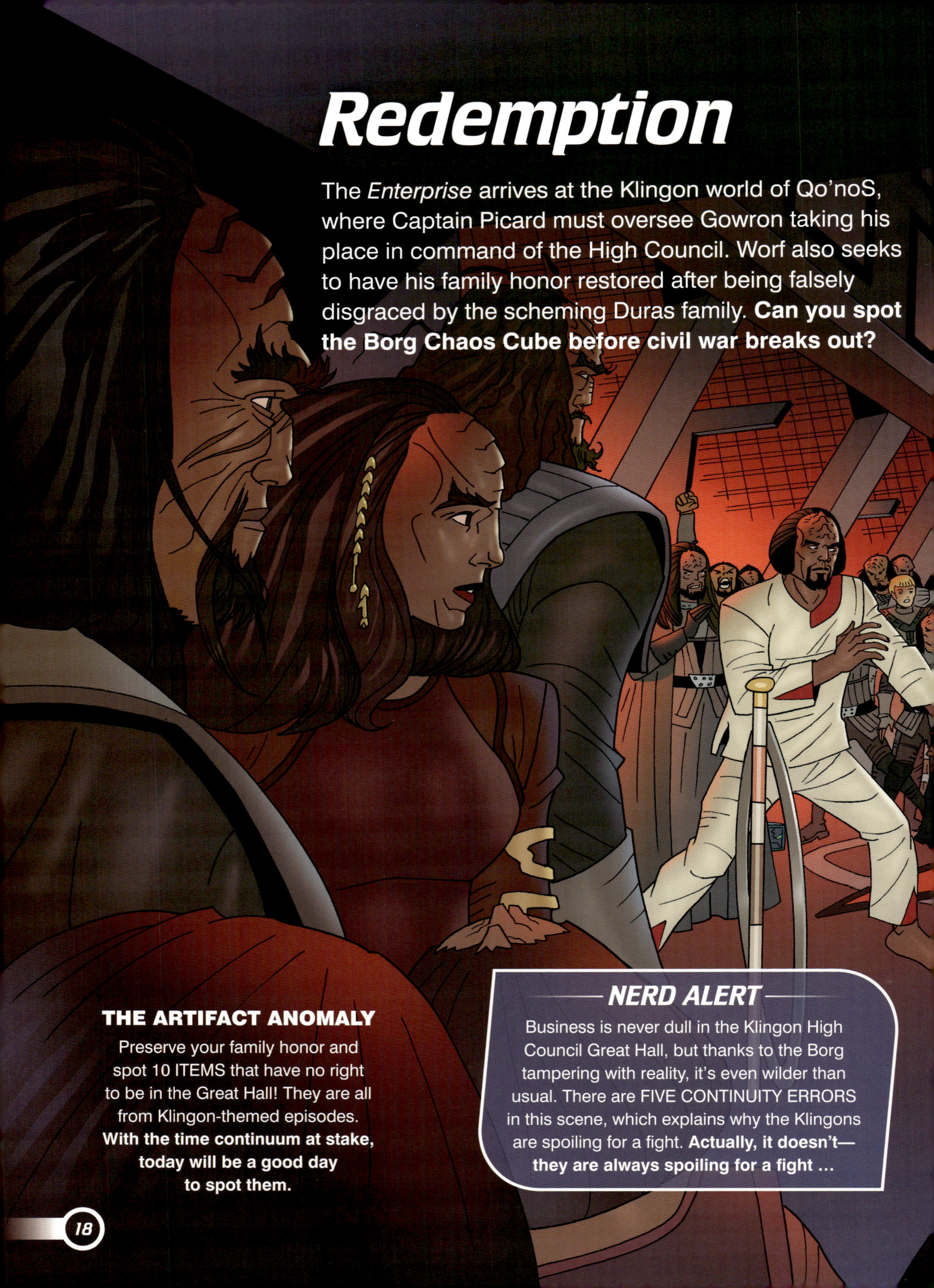

Redemption

The *Enterprise* arrives at the Klingon world of Qo'noS, where Captain Picard must oversee Gowron taking his place in command of the High Council. Worf also seeks to have his family honor restored after being falsely disgraced by the scheming Duras family. **Can you spot the Borg Chaos Cube before civil war breaks out?**

THE ARTIFACT ANOMALY

Preserve your family honor and spot 10 ITEMS that have no right to be in the Great Hall! They are all from Klingon-themed episodes. **With the time continuum at stake, today will be a good day to spot them.**

NERD ALERT

Business is never dull in the Klingon High Council Great Hall, but thanks to the Borg tampering with reality, it's even wilder than usual. There are FIVE CONTINUITY ERRORS in this scene, which explains why the Klingons are spoiling for a fight. **Actually, it doesn't—they are always spoiling for a fight …**

SUPER QUIBBLE
Can you spot the special
talking point?

Unification

Picard and Data have traveled to the planet Romulus to discover why Ambassador Spock has seemingly defected there. In fact, Spock is quite logically trying to bring unity to the Romulan and Vulcan peoples. **Naturally, unity is hard to come by… especially if that Borg Chaos Cube keeps meddling…**

SUPER QUIBBLE
Can you spot the special talking point?

THE ARTIFACT ANOMALY

One can begin to reshape the landscape with a single flower, but this scene has been reshaped with 10 ITEMS that should not be there. **They are all from episodes with guest stars and familiar faces …**

NERD ALERT

Reality is being disunified by the Borg, leading to FIVE CONTINUITY ERRORS. There might be movie-related time-twists, or simple errors of costume and make-up. **It's time for some cowboy diplomacy, so get busy, original-series-style, and save the day.**

Encounter at Farpoint /All Good Things

NERD ALERT

We have to save humanity from the FIVE CONTINUITY ERRORS in this mind-boggling mash-up of the first and last *STAR TREK: THE NEXT GENERATION* adventures. **They could be characters in the wrong scene, or the wrong version of characters in the right scene!**

Does mankind deserve to survive? Q is still holding court, and a spatial anomaly is threatening to rewrite time and wipe out the whole Alpha Quadrant. That's where you live. **Prove we can pass Q's test by spotting the Borg Chaos Cube before all good things come to an end!**

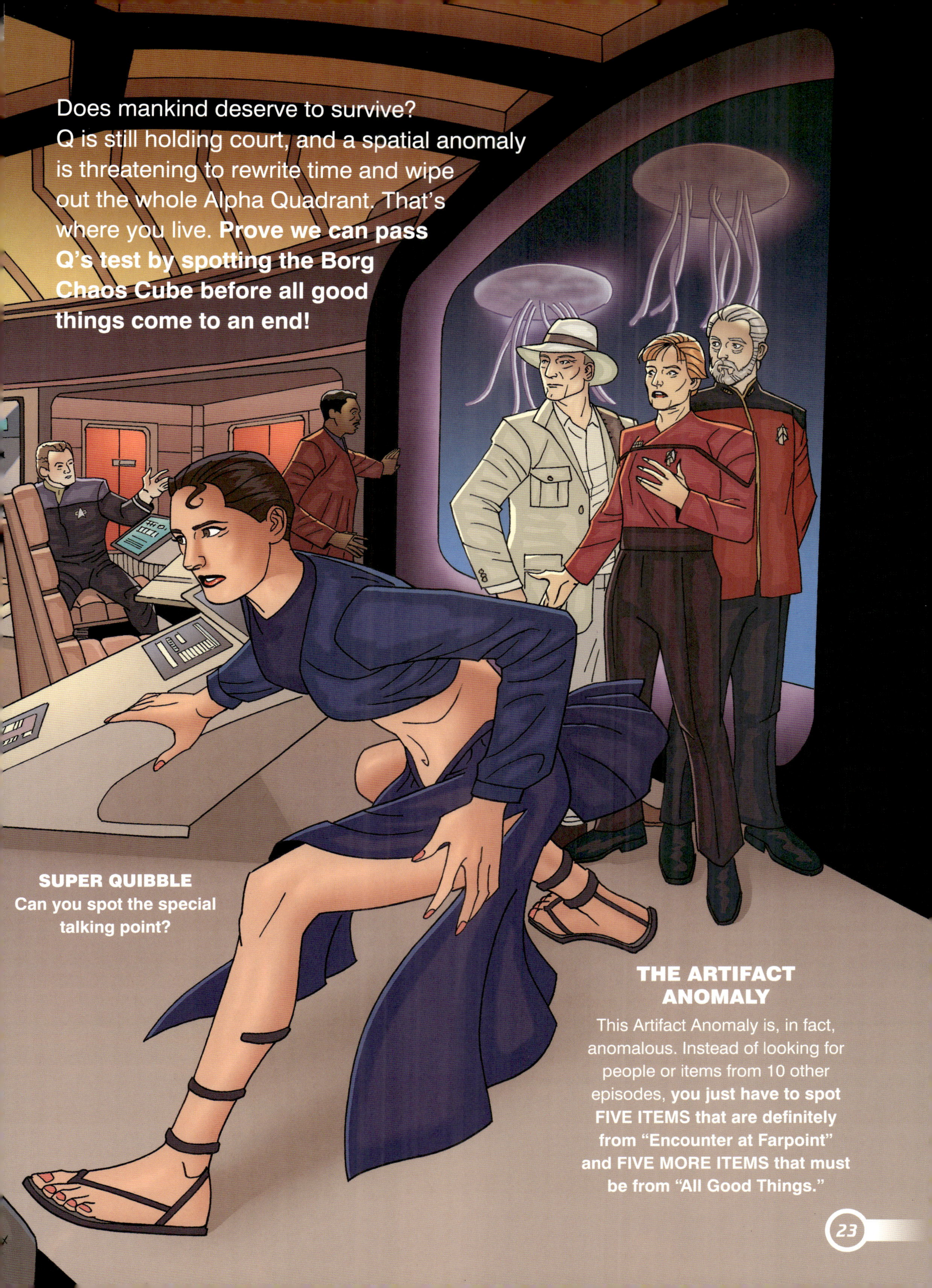

SUPER QUIBBLE

Can you spot the special talking point?

THE ARTIFACT ANOMALY

This Artifact Anomaly is, in fact, anomalous. Instead of looking for people or items from 10 other episodes, **you just have to spot FIVE ITEMS that are definitely from "Encounter at Farpoint" and FIVE MORE ITEMS that must be from "All Good Things."**

ANSWERS

The Big Goodbye (S1.12)

Greetings, fellow nerds, your quest for the ultimate prize of 2364 points awaits you. We begin our trek through *STAR TREK: THE NEXT GENERATION* with this popular episode, written by Tracy Tormé—yes, son of the great Mel. Prepare to enter the holodeck …

CATCH THE CUBE: D7

NERD ALERT: FIVE CONTINUITY ERRORS

1. E6. Riker is lying, shot on the ground, instead of the historian, Dr. Whalen, who should be there.

2. B5. Gangster, Cyrus Redblock is pointing a gun at Picard—this never happened. Redblock's menace is always understated. Actor Lawrence Tierney also played the Regent of Palamar in the *STAR TREK: DEEP SPACE NINE* episode, "Business as Usual" (S5.18).

3. C2. Mr. Spock did appear gangster-style in the original series, in "A Piece of the Action" (S2.17) but did not pop up in this episode. Leonard Nimoy did later reprise his role as Spock for the two-parter "Unification" (S5.7—8).

4. C6. Beverly has some chewing gum in her hand, but this happened in an earlier scene.

5. A6. Badgey should certainly not be there. The chirpy tutorial hologram first appeared in the *STAR TREK: LOWER DECKS* episode "Terminal Provocations" (S1.6). A parody of supposedly helpful but annoying software assistance, the character has become a kind of series mascot. He is voiced by Jack McBrayer, famous as Kenneth from *30 Rock*.

TEN OUT-OF-CONTEXT ITEMS FROM OTHER HOLODECK EPISODES

6. B4. Here's Data as he appeared in "A Fistful of Datas" (S6.8). Data should be in the scene, but not in this Wild West get-up.

7. D6. Minuet from "11001001" (S1.15) is looking concerned for Riker. Played by Carolyn McCormick, Minuet was a super-sophisticated holodeck character created by a race called the Bynars to distract Riker while they took over the *Enterprise*. Guess what? It worked. She was cleverly referenced as Min Riker in "Future Imperfect" (S4.8), when an alien, Barash, created a fake future for Riker to live in. Drawing on Riker's memories to create the illusion, Barash did not realize that Minuet had only ever been a hologram and could not have ever been his real wife or given birth to a son! Still, they made a cute family.

8. D1. Meet Picard's holo-horse from "Pen Pals" (S2.15).

9. C3. Picard is holding a Klingon pain stick from "The Icarus Factor" (S2.14). It is used in the holodeck during Worf's Second Rite of Ascension.

10. B3. Holographic Data's flamboyant hat from "Hollow Pursuits" (S3.21) is on a hat stand. For this you can thank Lieutenant Barclay, who created his own versions of the crew members for holodeck fantasies.

11. C3. The combadge from Riker's fake future in "Future Imperfect" (S4.8) is worn by Picard.

12. D2. The Ferengi, Bok, used this forbidden thought-maker device against Picard in "The Battle" (S1.9).

13. F3. This musical instrument is from Picard's simulation of a past date he never attended in "We'll Always Have Paris" (S1.24). The old romantic. Please don't ask us how it works!

14. B7. This model of the *Enterprise* from *STAR TREK* was seen in the episode "Booby Trap" (S3.6), in which Geordi created a holographic copy of Drafting Room 5 at the Utopia Planitia Fleet Yards to help him solve a problem. He also fell for a hologram of Dr. Leah Brahms, who designed warp engines.

15. B5. The sign from Charnock's Comedy Cabaret in "The Outrageous Okona" (S2.4) is on the wall. Data used the holodeck to try to learn how to deliver jokes. "Take my Worf … please!" The club's name is a reference to Ed Charnock Jnr., who was a painter in the show's art department.

Super Quibble: E2. On the floor is a copy of "Amazing Detective Stories." This is the publication in which Dixon Hill's adventures were said to appear. It was only mentioned in dialogue, and Data evidently scanned its contents via computer, but no actual book ever appeared on screen.

1
2
3
4
5
6
7
A
B
C
D
E
F
Charnock's
COMEDY
Cabaret

The Defector (S3.10)

Our space scene features that dangerous location the Neutral Zone, into which the *Enterprise* was lured by the scheming Romulans, using the elaborate plan of feeding misinformation to the defecting Admiral Jarok. We have taken the opportunity to test you with an array of starships, creatures, and weird space phenomena … but hey, you chose to stray into the Neutral Zone …

CATCH THE CUBE: F5.

NERD ALERT: FIVE CONTINUITY ERRORS

1. C6. The Klingons did turn up to help the *Enterprise*, but not in the Ship of the Dead from *STAR TREK: DISCOVERY* (S1.1).
2. C4. The Romulans did not fire their disruptors.
3. C3. The *Enterprise* should not have *DISCOVERY*-era repair drones attending it.
4. F5. The Klingon ship should not be battle-damaged.
5. C1. There should not be a Romulan bird-of-prey from *STAR TREK*.

TEN OUT-OF-CONTEXT ITEMS FROM OTHER SPACE SCENES

6. C5. Did you recognize Tin Man from "Tin Man" (S3.20)? It was neither tin nor man, but a sentient spaceship called Gomtuu.
7. E4. Passing by is the Gekli creature from "Galaxy's Child" (S4.16).
8. A5. You probably recognized the dangerous fronds of the Crystalline Entity from "Silicon Avatar" (S5.4). This was an ally of Data's evil twin, Lore.
9. E2. This giant space rock was a key location in "The Pegasus" (S7.12).
10. D5. A toughie. Did you realize that this glow wasn't a random space effect but the space time fissure that caused so much trouble in "Parallels" (S7.11)?
11. F4. Did you spot the Pakled ship from "Samaritan Snare" (S2.17)? The technology-snaffling aliens reappeared with mightier vessels in *STAR TREK: LOWER DECKS*, "No Small Parts" (S1.10).
12. B6. Perhaps you recalled the distinctive look of this Mercenary Raider from "Gambit," Part 1 (S7.4).
13. C3. This is the Relay Station from "Aquiel" (S6.13).
14. D1. You may remember the probe that zapped Picard in "The Inner Light" (S5.25) and led him to experience a totally different life on the planet Kataan, as a man called Kamin. While that society was now long gone, Jean-Luc did learn to play the flute, a skill he retained to the astonishment of all that knew him. An acclaimed story from writer Morgan Gendel.
15. C5. This revolving door will let you into a mysterious hotel in space. It's from "The Royale" (S2.12), a memorably quirky early tale with a hint of old-school sci-fi pulp mystery.

Super Quibble: C4. This spaceship is from *STAR TREK: THE ANIMATED SERIES*. It's from "The Pirates of Orion" (S2.1). You truly deserve the ridiculously high quibble-points if you recognized it! The episode was memorable for McCoy referring to Spock as a "pointy-eared encyclopedia."

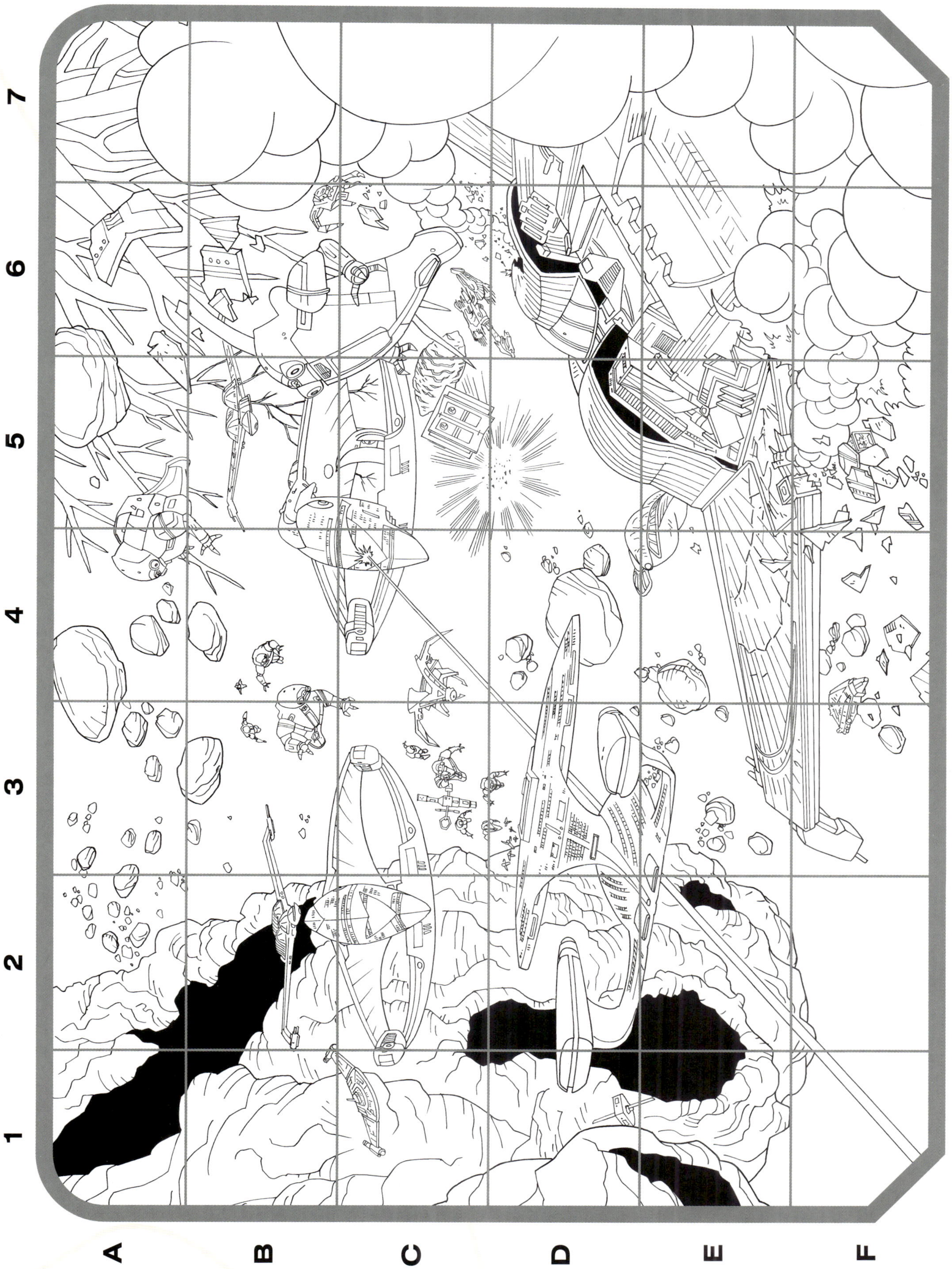
1
2
3
4
5
6
7
A
B
C
D
E
F

Sarek (S3.23)

This episode is a true landmark in the history of *STAR TREK: THE NEXT GENERATION*. When Mark Lenard reprised his role as Spock's father, it demonstrated the new show was confident enough to fully embrace its past. On a sadder note, Sarek's frailty in this story is said to reflect the similar state of *TREK* creator Gene Roddenberry at the time.

CATCH THE CUBE: D3

NERD ALERT: FIVE CONTINUITY ERRORS

1. B7. Sarek should not be in Ten Forward. His emotions triggered this scene, but he was completely oblivious to it.
2. C2. Sarek's wife was also not in the scene. And if she had been, it certainly wouldn't have been his first wife Amanda (Jane Wyatt) from *STAR TREK*. She had been replaced by Sarek's second wife, also a human, Perrin, played by Joanna Miles.
3. C4. Worf enters with a drawn phaser—this did not happen, although Worf was portrayed as trigger-happy in the early days, even attempting to shoot an image of Q on a screen, in "Encounter at Farpoint" (S1.1).
4. C3. Guinan should not be serving behind the bar, she was not in this episode, though she had joined the crew in "The Child" (S2.1).
5. E1. Picard did shed tears in this episode, but only during his emotional mind melding with Sarek, which only Dr. Crusher witnessed.

TEN OUT-OF-CONTEXT ITEMS FROM OTHER AMBASSADOR, EMISSARY AND REPRESENTATIVE-THEMED EPISODES

6. C5. Dathon from Darmok is in the background (S5.2). We hope this answer leaves your eyes uncovered and your arms wide.
7. D2. Kamala (Famke Janssen) from "The Perfect Mate" sits with Picard (S5.21).
8. C7. Ishara Yar, Tasha's sister from "Legacy" is in the bar (S4.6).
9. C4. T'Pel from "Data's Day" is in the scene (S4.11). This is a tough spot for you, but the Vulcan traitor does have very distinctive headgear!
10. F4. This is a Selay, one of the memorable reptile people from "Lonely Among Us" (S1.11).
11. E1. Did you spot this neural parasite from "Conspiracy" (S1.25)? Okay, so it's not exactly an ambassador, but we couldn't bear to leave it out!
12. C1. Lwaxana Troi, Betazoid ambassador and Deanna's extrovert mother, appears as we saw her in "Dark Page" (S7.7), one of her more poignant episodes. This is actress Majel Barrett, wife of Gene Roddenberry, who played Number One in the pilot episode "The Cage," Nurse Chapel in *STAR TREK*, Lwaxana in *STAR TREK: THE NEXT GENERATION* and *STAR TREK: DEEP SPACE NINE*. She also appeared as the voice of the starship computers up to *STAR TREK: ENTERPRISE*, and in the movie *STAR TREK* (2009), so true fans will know her well!
13. C3. The "delightful" Betazoid gift box from "Haven" (S1.11).
14. D7. This chicken appeared in the episode "Up the Long Ladder" (S2.18) and was a member, perhaps a representative, of the Bringloidi colony. This episode is often referred to as "Send In The Clones" by fans as it was a cutely suggested alternative title (that gave the plot away).
15. D2. Ah, who can forget the sweet buffet from "Liaisons" (S7.2)? Lucky Iyaaran Ambassador, Loquel, was introduced to desserts by Deanna.

Super Quibble: B4. On the far wall we see a family portrait of Michael Burnham, Spock, and Sybok (*STAR TREK V: THE FINAL FRONTIER*), all raised by Sarek and Amanda. Some mystery hangs over their past as a family, as Spock never mentioned Burnham in *STAR TREK*, or Sybok. Also Burnham and Spock never mentioned Sybok in *STAR TREK: DISCOVERY* and Spock and Sybok certainly never reminisced about life with Burnham in *STAR TREK V: THE FINAL FRONTIER*. The episode "Sarek" was of great significance to Spock fans, as it was the first time his name was spoken in *STAR TREK: THE NEXT GENERATION* and gave hope for his return.

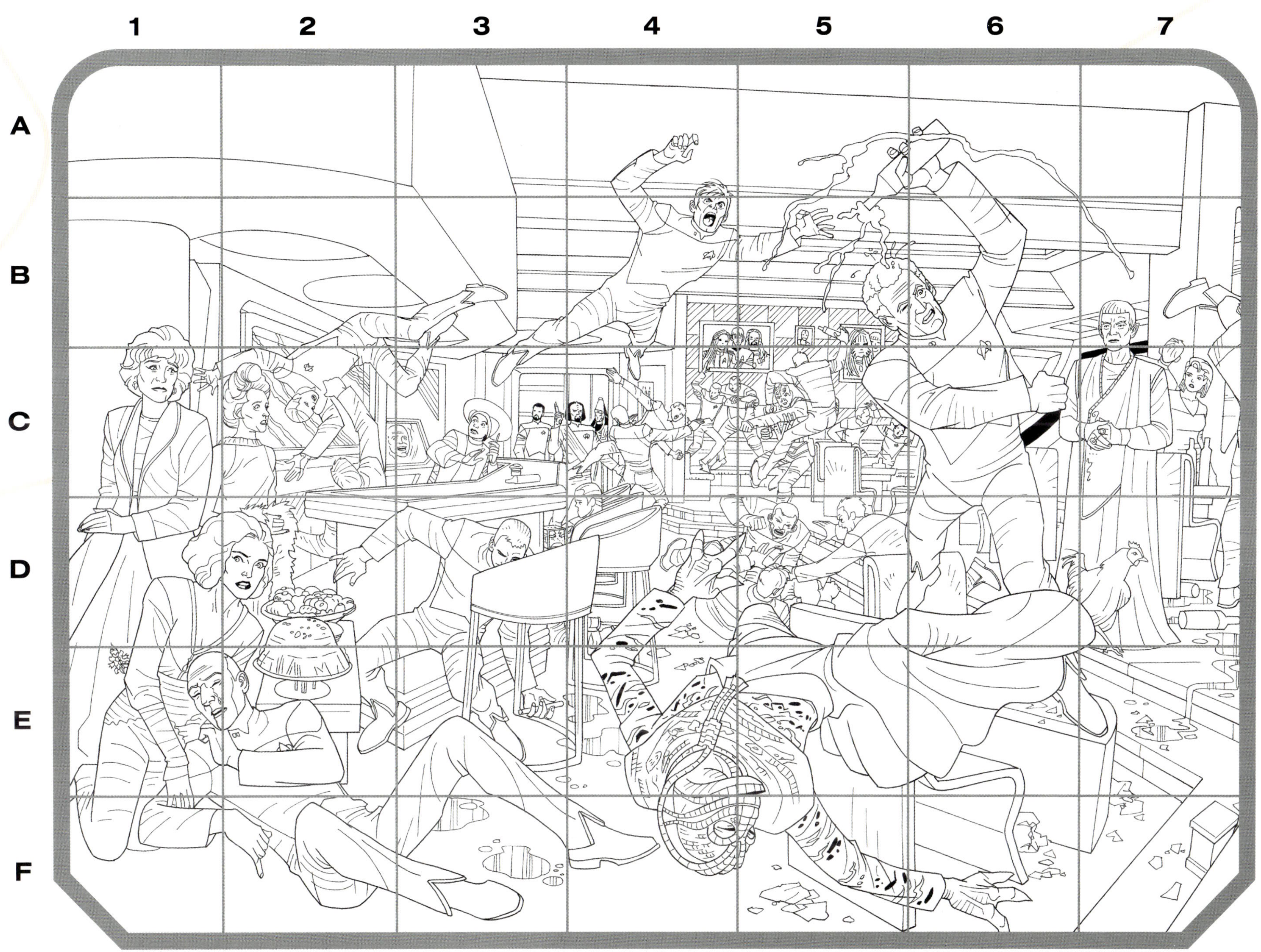
1
2
3
4
5
6
7
A
B
C
D
E
F

The Best of Both Worlds (S3.26–S4.1)

Regarded as one of the high points of *STAR TREK: THE NEXT GENERATION*, the two-part story brought back the popular bad guys, the Borg, and gave us Picard as Locutus of Borg. Some fan rumors have claimed that the dramatic storyline of Jean-Luc's abduction was there to allow for the possibility of Patrick Stewart and Michael Piller (exec producer) leaving the series … luckily that did not happen.

CATCH THE CUBE: C7

NERD ALERT: FIVE CONTINUITY ERRORS

1. C4. The Borg Queen from *STAR TREK: FIRST CONTACT* was not in the story.
2. C3. Picard was only partly assimilated at first, and when the crew came to rescue him did not have a half-face mask.
3. C5. Crusher should not be wearing her uniform from *STAR TREK: INSURRECTION*.
4. C7. You'll kick yourself for this: Worf's sash is the wrong way round. Treat yourself to a Klingon howl if you missed it.
5. C5. A Borg is checking its cell phone. Wouldn't happen. Borgs are part of a collective mind and anyway are not allowed to have cell phones at work.

TEN OUT-OF-CONTEXT ITEMS FROM OTHER BORG, ROBOT, AND ARTIFICIAL SENTIENCE EPISODES

6. C4. Hugh from "I Borg" (S5.23) should not be in the scene. Hugh was also revived for *STAR TREK: PICARD*, and once again played by Jonathan Del Arco.
7. B3. Did you spot Lore, as he appeared in "Descent", Part 2 (S7.1)? Lore, Data's evil twin, was first seen in "Datalore" (S1.13), after some difficulty finding an actor to play the part. (That bit was a lie.)
8. C1. This is the first Borg ever seen on screen, from the classic episode "Q Who" (S2.16). This Borg was not in this story, and certainly not re-enacting his first appearance. "Q Who" is seen by some as a turning point for *STAR TREK: THE NEXT GENERATION*, at last providing the new series with its own formidable enemies.
9. C3. This is one of the toughest spots in the book, but above Picard is the gadget that helped convert him back to a human in part two—and should not be on the Borg Cube.
10. B4. We hope you spotted the cute Exocomp from "The Quality of Life" (S6.9). The Exocomps were revived for *STAR TREK: LOWER DECKS*, in "No Small Parts" (S1.10), in which a female of the species named herself Peanut Hamper in a bid to avoid sounding robotic.
11. C1. Here we find Lal, Data's daughter, from the heart-rending episode "The Offspring" (S3.16), memorably played by Hallie Todd. This was the first episode to be directed by Jonathan Frakes, who has gone on to a long directorial career across the franchise.
12. D2. This is the sentient life form the *Enterprise* produced in "Emergence" (S7.23). It is always an emotional moment when a spaceship has a baby.
13. C6. Countess Regina (Stephanie Beacham) is among the away team. Moriarty's girlfriend was a form of holographic life created in the *Enterprise*'s holodeck. She brought out the better side in Sherlock Holmes's arch enemy, which is no mean feat. This was how she appeared in "Ship in a Bottle" (S2.3).
14. B7. Did you remember the Echo Papa 607 weapon from "Arsenal of Freedom" (S1.21)? It was part of an intelligent weapons system on the planet Minos.
15. D7. We mentioned the episode "Datalore" above, and this spare android head, found in Dr. Soong's lab, is from that show.

Super Quibble: D5. Could Seven of Nine possibly have been involved in this incident? Although she first appeared in *STAR TREK: VOYAGER*, "Scorpion", Part 2 (S4.1) as a matter of continuity she had been assimilated by this stage. Take the points if you spotted her and quibbled it!

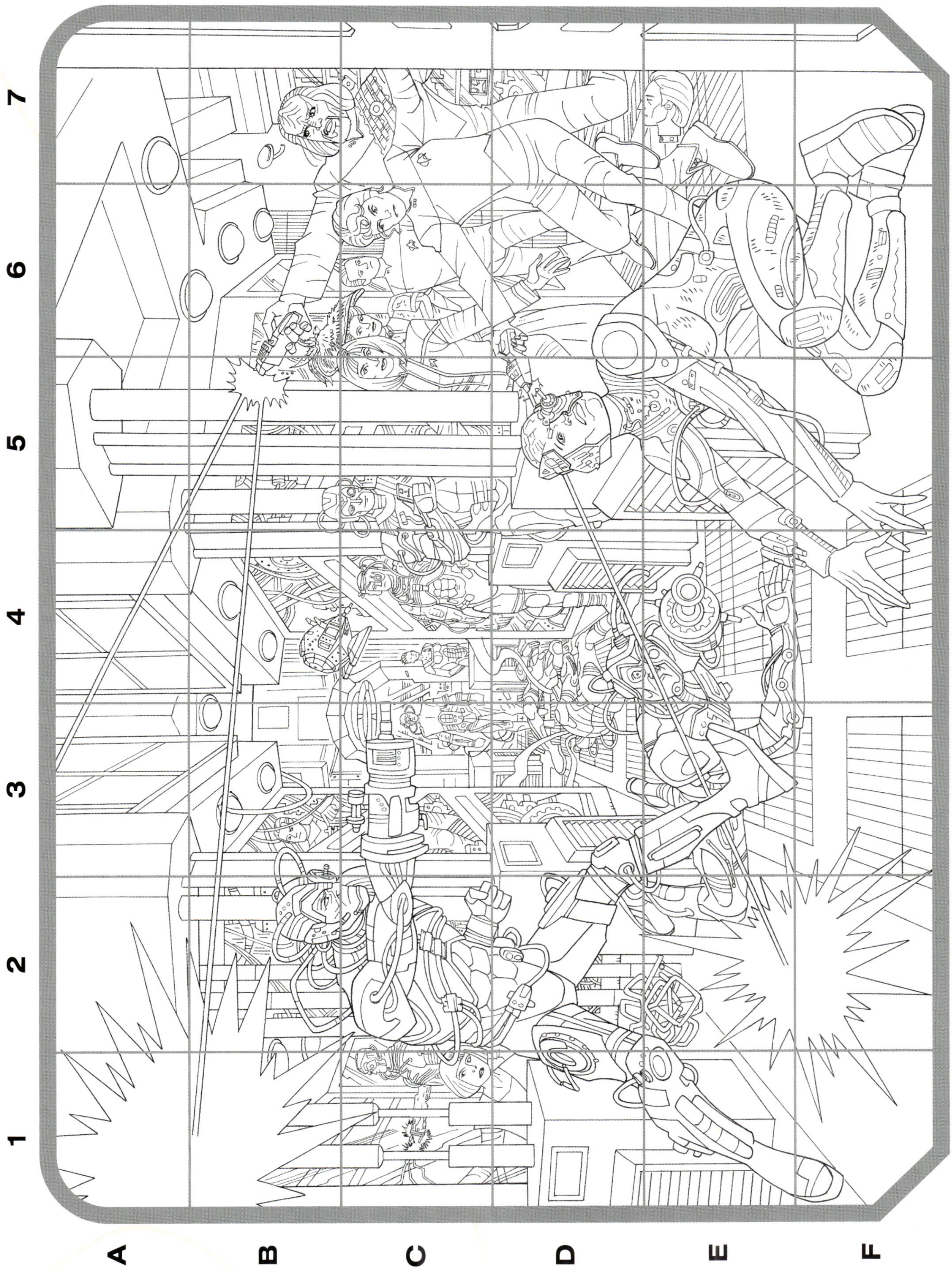

1
2
3
4
5
6
7
A
B
C
D
E
F

Qpid (S4.20)

Zounds! It's time to journey to the city of Nottingham in Merrie Olde Englande as the all-powerful being Q attempts to explore the subject of romance—as part of his ongoing mentorship/torment of Jean-Luc. Q always aimed to liven up the lives of Picard and crew, and this story hit the target.

CATCH THE CUBE: E4.

NERD ALERT: FIVE CONTINUITY ERRORS

1. B6. Vash should not be in her poolside holiday outfit from "Captain's Holiday" (S3.19).
2. C7. Q should not be wearing his robes from "Encounter at Farpoint" (S1.1): he was attired as the Sheriff of Nottingham.
3. B4. Picard should not be sword-fighting with his walking stick from *STAR TREK: PICARD* (S1.1).
4. B1. Data did get hit by an arrow, but it was earlier in the episode. It was fired by Deanna Troi!
5. B6. Geordi (as Alan-a-Dale) could not be playing his mandolin in the fight scene. Music-lover, Worf, smashed it earlier (well, he prefers Klingon opera).

TEN OUT-OF-CONTEXT ITEMS FROM OTHER Q AND ALL-POWERFUL BEING EPISODES

6. D2. Did you recognize female Q, Amanda Rogers—and her puppy—from "True Q" (S6.6)?
7. C5. This soldier is from "Hide and Q" (S1.10).
8. C3. This Nausicaan appeared in "Tapestry" (S6.15), the episode in which Q gave Picard a chance to revisit some old mistakes—and make even bigger ones.
9. B6. Our old friend, the Mariarchi from "Deja Q" (S3.13), was adding party atmosphere to the bridge of the *Enterprise* (unwanted by Picard).
10. D7. Who can forget the eerie visage of Nagilum, the all-powerful menace from "Where Silence Has Lease" (S2.2)?
11. B4. This is a tricky connection, but this is the frame of flowers that Wesley Crusher damaged in "Justice" (S1.8)—the episode in which the Edo race had an all-powerful god.
12. C4. The ever-unpopular, but all-powerful-seeming Armus creature from "Skin of Evil" (S1.23). This evil oil slick killed Tasha Yar—a fate determined by the fact that Denise Crosby had decided to leave the show.
13. E1. A Klingon Targ. What's the connection? It appeared during "Where No One Has Gone Before" (S1.6), the episode that introduced the being known as the Traveler.
14. B2. This is the symbol of the god-like Masaka from the episode "Masks" (S7.17).
15. B7. Did you spot Ardra, the potent pest from "Devil's Due" (S4.13)? She did appear in Starfleet uniform at one point, which was thrown in to throw you.

Super Quibble: B5. Fans of *STAR TREK* will immediately recognize the all-powerful Squire of Gothos from the episode of the same name (S1.17). The Squire has been retrospectively regarded as a "Q" by fans and referred to as such in the expanded universe. William Campbell, the actor who played Trelane, also portrayed the Klingon, Captain Koloth, in the classic "The Trouble with Tribbles" in *STAR TREK* (S2.15).

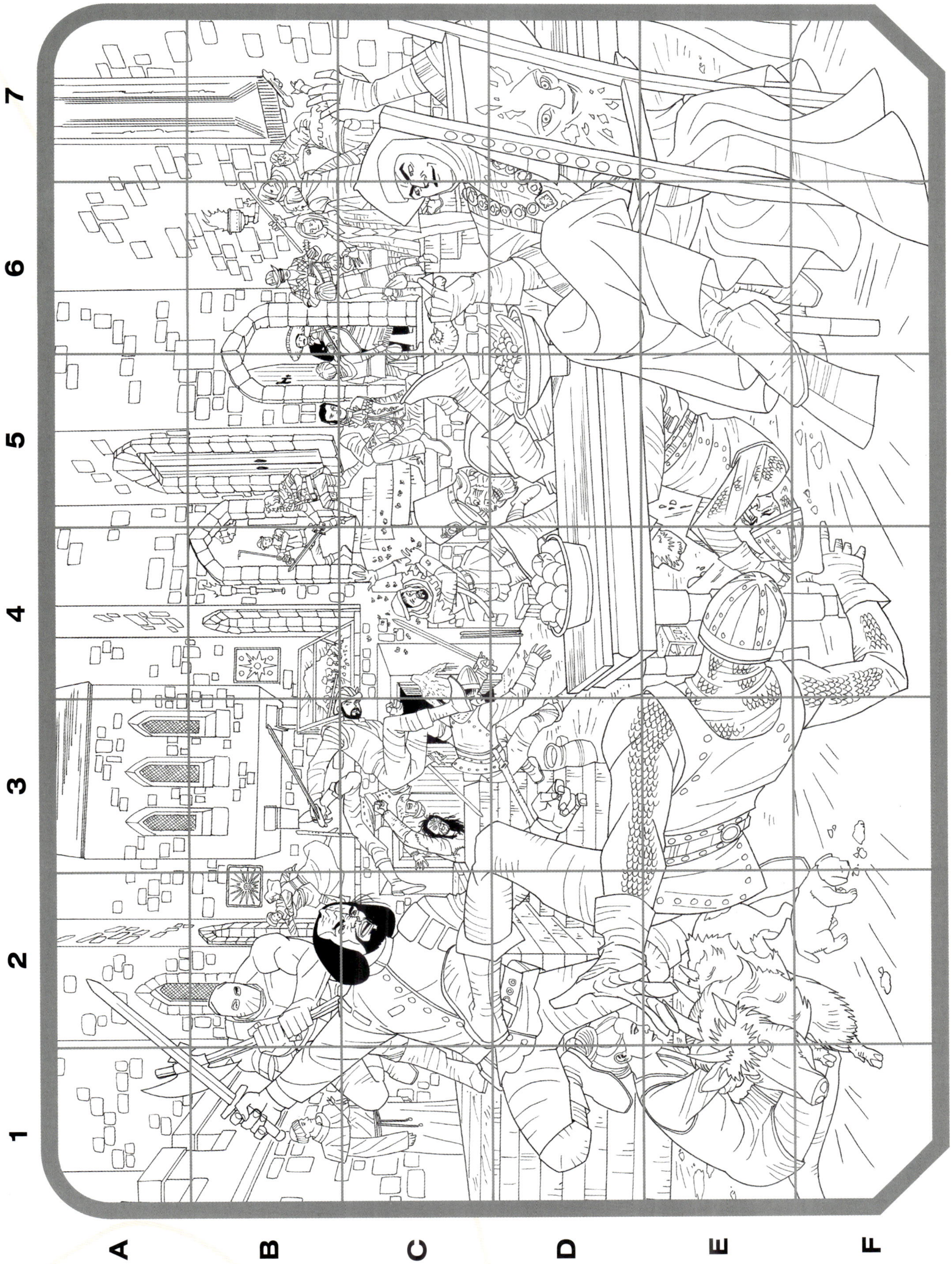

1
2
3
4
5
6
7
A
B
C
D
E
F

Redemption *(S4.26–S5.1)*

This Worf spectacular, written by Klingon expert Ronald D. Moore, wove together plot strands set up in "Sins of the Father" (S3.17), which he also wrote. The story also introduced the scheming Romulan, Sela, offspring of an alternative-timeline Tasha Yar, giving Denise Crosby a way back into the series, after Tasha was killed off in "Skin of Evil" (S1.23).

CATCH THE CUBE: D3

NERD ALERT: FIVE CONTINUITY ERRORS

1. C3. Worf should not be wearing his white training robe from early in "Redemption," Part 1 (S4.26).

2. C4. Sela, while in this tale, was not in any Great Hall scenes.

3. B6—7. The Duras sisters, while always around where there is trouble, were not in the Great Hall at this time either.

4. C5. Picard should not be sitting on the throne in the Great Hall—that is a bit too much of an honor, even for him. He was Arbiter of Succession, not the actual leader.

5. C4. Toral should not have the ceremonial knife, as it was never given to him, which is just as well.

TEN OUT-OF-CONTEXT ITEMS FROM OTHER KLINGON EPISODES

6. C2. Did you spot K'Ehleyr from "The Emissary" (S2.20)? She was played by the popular Suzie Plakson, and there was much howling when she was killed off in "Reunion" (S4.7).

7. E5. Worf's son Alexander is in the scene, as he appeared in "Cost of Living" (S5.10). He first appeared in "Reunion" (S4.7) and became a regular face on the show.

8. A7. Commander Kurn is looking on, taking a great interest, as he is Worf's younger brother. This is how he appeared in "Sins of the Father".

9. C5. This intriguing-looking sculpture is actually a hologram of Worf's spine as seen in "Ethics" (S5.16).

10. C7. Remember Korris from "Heart of Glory" (S1.20)? Top marks for identifying him in death-howl mode.

11. E6. This Gilvo creature is from "New Ground" (S5.10). The Klingon connection? Alexander and these creatures were placed in danger during an accident aboard the ship caused by the experimental new Soliton Wave.

12. D3. Even Klingons like to play sometimes. These items are from the game played in the Romulan prison colony in "Birthright", Part II (S6.17).

13. C7. Who can forget Riker eating gagh in "A Matter of Honor" (S2.8)? He seemed to love it, but he wasn't invited along to eat any in "Redemption!"

14. C5. Whom do we seek? Kahless! Well, you have found him. This depiction was on the wall of the Temple of Boreth, in "Rightful Heir" (S6.23).

15. B7. Okay, this is another toughie. This mind-control device was seen in "The Mind's Eye," with Geordi's head in it! (S4.24) He was programmed to kill the Klingon Governor (but didn't). Yay.

Super Quibble: C5. Did you spot the original-series-style Klingon in the background? This type of Klingon clashed repeatedly with Kirk and co., but seemed to have mysteriously vanished by the time of *STAR TREK: THE NEXT GENERATION*. The Klingons were restyled to look more menacing in *STAR TREK: THE MOTION PICTURE*, and the restyle was kept for *STAR TREK: THE NEXT GENERATION*. It was later revealed that genetic experiments had caused Klingons some limited mutation into more "human" appearance for a short while. Oh, the horror.

1
2
3
4
5
6
7
A
B
C
D
E
F

Unification (S5.7–8)

At last, Mr. Spock appeared in *STAR TREK: THE NEXT GENERATION*, and in a spectacular two-part tale. All the original series cast were now making *STAR TREK* movies, and this story was broadcast just weeks before the release of *STAR TREK VI: THE UNDISCOVERED COUNTRY*, and even refers to its events. Nimoy accepted a pay cut to revive his classic role.

CATCH THE CUBE: D7.

NERD ALERT: FIVE CONTINUITY ERRORS

1. C5. Spock should not be dressed as he was for *STAR TREK: THE MOTION PICTURE*!
2. C5. Picard should not still be in his Romulan disguise. When Sela and her forces sprang their trap, Jean-Luc was in Starfleet uniform.
3. B3. Data did not use the Vulcan nerve pinch on Sela until later.
4. C4. Kirk did not appear in "Unification," but he did appear three years later in *STAR TREK GENERATIONS*, William Shatner's last appearance in the role to date.
5. A5 (and throughout). Romulan guards should not be in their stylish sixties uniforms.

TEN OUT-OF-CONTEXT ITEMS FROM OTHER GUEST STAR AND FAMILIAR FACE EPISODES

6. B6. Did you spot Scotty as he appeared in "Relics" (S6.4)? The injured arm is a giveaway. Not only was "Relics" James Doohan's last TV appearance as Scotty, but it was also his most demanding, as the character had never had so many lines before. There were tears on set from the production team at his sentimental return.
7. A7. This is a tricky one, but did you spot the famous face of Moriarty, lying unconscious? Appearing here as he did in "Elementary, Dear Data" (S2.3), the Sherlock Holmes villain made an unlikely transformation into *TREK* baddie, via the magic of the Holodeck. Actor Daniel Davis gave him a perceptive, relatable quality, and he returned memorably for "Ship in a Bottle" (S6.12).
8. D7. Einstein is here, contemplating the infinite, as ever. Played by Jim Norton, Einstein was conjured in the holodeck by Reg Barclay in "The Nth Degree" (S4.19) and Data in "Descent" (S6.26) in a scene that also included Isaac Newton and the real Stephen Hawking. Genius.
9. E4. Quark is where the action is, as usual! He appeared in "Firstborn" (S7.21). *STAR TREK: DEEP SPACE NINE* had been on our screens since January 1993, starting halfway through season six of *STAR TREK: THE NEXT GENERATION*, and so Quark was already familiar to fans by this point.
10. B6. This is probably the hardest spot in the book, but Mark Twain's straw hat is here from "Time's Arrow" (S5.26). Give yourself the points if you thought: "Hmm, what's that hat doing there?"
11. B4. Admiral McCoy is here from "Encounter at Farpoint" (S1.1). Although 137 years old, he made light of his age, saying: "What's so damn troublesome about not having died?"
12. D6. Meet Devor from the episode "Starship Mine" (S6.18). Why should we want to meet a trilithium thief? Well, he was played by Tim Russ, who went on to become Tuvok in *STAR TREK: VOYAGER*.
13. B3. This Carolus Chess game is from the episode "Ménage à Troi" (S3.24), in which actor Ethan Phillips plays a Ferengi. Phillips is, of course, Neelix in *STAR TREK: VOYAGER*. An immediate Starfleet Academy scholarship if you made the connection!
14. A4. Another super-tricky one—this device is the field generator that Dr. Bashir from *STAR TREK: DEEP SPACE NINE* was working on when he met Data in "Birthright, Part I," (S6.16). Actually, give yourself a point if you looked at the device and thought: "I bet that was in some episode or other!"
15. C7. Sarek has dropped by from the episode "Sarek" (S3.23).

Super Quibble: A5. Did you spot this Romulan Commander? He should not be there as he is from *STAR TREK* "Balance of Terror" (S1.14). Give yourself the points if you knew he was played by Mark Lenard, who also played Sarek, who is also in the scene.

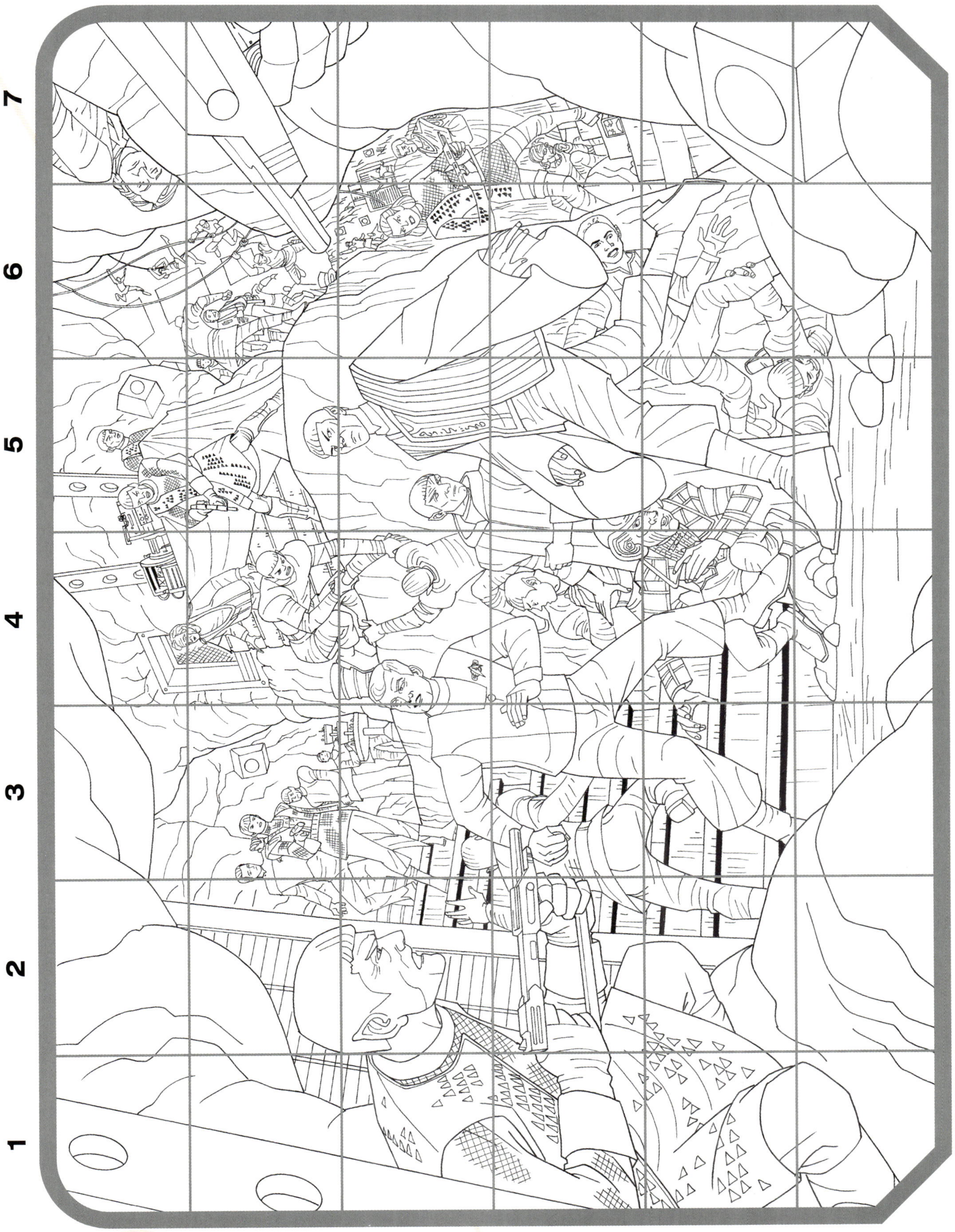

1
2
3
4
5
6
7
A
B
C
D
E
F

Encounter at Farpoint/All Good Things (S1.1 & S7.25–6)

The *Enterprise*-D begins (and ends) its adventures in this marvelous mash-up of the first episode and the last. The intriguing idea to mix the beginning with the end was central to the concept of the big finale, so don't blame us if it gets confusing. Blame top *TREK* writers Brannon Braga and Ronald D. Moore…

CATCH THE CUBE: C1.

**NERD ALERT:
FIVE CONTINUITY ERRORS**

1. C2. Doctor Pulaski should not be here as she was not in the story. Diana Muldaur became the ship's doctor for season two, when Dr. Crusher (Gates McFadden) did not have her contract renewed (temporarily). Muldaur was a popular replacement, and was a natural choice for a doctor, having played both Dr. Ann Mulhall and Dr. Miranda Jones in *STAR TREK*. Someone in casting must have had her down as a doctor …

2. B6. There were other versions of Picard in this tale, but not as he appeared in *STAR TREK: PICARD* "Absolute Candor" (S1.4).

3. C5. Denise Crosby did reprise her role as Tasha for the reshot "Farpoint" scenes, but was not seen in the outfit she wore in "The Naked Now" (S1.2).

4. C4. O'Brien (Colm Meaney) did return for the episode, but not in his later uniform from *STAR TREK: DEEP SPACE NINE*.

5. C2. Despite the time-traveling shenanigans of this story, the red lift doors from the bridge of *STAR TREK* did not make a guest appearance.

TEN ITEMS TO BE IDENTIFIED AS FROM "ENCOUNTER AT FARPOINT" (EAF) OR "ALL GOOD THINGS" (AGT) …

6. B3. The frozen crewman is from EAF. His name was Lieutenant Torres and fans will be pleased to hear he was thawed out successfully and later returned to duty. Torres was played by stunt man Jimmy Ortega.

7. B3. This version of Q as 16th-century ship's captain is from EAF. Actor John de Lancie actually made a special request to appear in the last episode, and was told he was in it already, with the whole story built around him.

8. C2. Wesley Crusher (Wil Wheaton) sitting in the Captain's chair—is from EAF. The honor did not last long!

9. B6. These space jellyfish-like alien life forms were from the astonishing conclusion to EAF!

10. B4. Deanna Troi—in this memorable outfit—is definitely from EAF.

11. B2. Gray-haired Governor Worf is from AGT, which is said to take place in circa 2395.

12. B1. Data as Lucasian Professor of Mathematics at Cambridge University is from AGT. In his case, the streaked hair is an affectation.

13. C5. Geordi—without visor—is from AGT. This future version was retired from Starfleet and now a novelist. He was married to someone called Leah, which, if you have been following his career, you would hope to be Leah Brahms, the warp engine designer he had known in holographic form in "Booby Trap" (S3.6) and also as a harder-to-handle real human being, in "Galaxy's Child" (S4.16).

14. B7. Captain Beverly Picard of the U.S.S. *Pasteur* is from AGT. In this timeline she had married Jean-Luc and then separated, keeping his name.

15. B7. Admiral William T. Riker is from AGT, and though an old war horse was ever dependable in a crisis.

Super Quibble: C1. This screen mentions a crew member who never existed … but could have: the female Leslie Crusher. It was part of the early concept for the show that the bright youngster on the ship would be a girl, but this was later changed to Wesley. If you knew this, take the points!

1
2
3
4
5
6
7
A
B
C
D
E
F

HOW DID YOU DO?

Your Score

Well, the Borg have been defeated (if you didn't spot the cubes you could always look at the answers in the back and find them that way—it will annoy the Borg). But now it's time to see how well you know *STAR TREK: THE NEXT GENERATION*. Are you a genius-level performer like Barclay in "The Nth Degree" or more on the Pakled end of the scale?

2364 POINTS:

Congratulations! You have engaged the Borg and won! You are the ultimate fan, and possibly have some "Q" blood in your veins (if they have blood or veins).

500—2363:

Treat yourself to an Earl Grey, hot! You are as brainy as Picard and Guinan discussing the meaning of life on the holodeck with Einstein. Probably brainier.

200—499:

Intriguing! Your score is so impressive you could be some form of artificial intelligence. Be careful or Dr. Bruce Maddox will want to dissect your brain and build millions of you.

100—199:

It is possible, as Jean-Luc once said, to make no mistakes and lose. You have made a few, but you have won … our undying admiration! You have helped restore order to the cosmos.

0—99:

As Captain Picard once told Wesley, the only person you're truly competing against is yourself. So a low score this time means it'll be easier to beat yourself next time!

Published by Hero Collector Books,
a division of Eaglemoss. 2021
Premier Place, 2 & A Half Devonshire Square
London, EC2M 4UJ, UK
144, avenue Charles-de-Gaulle
92200 Neuilly-sur-Seine, France

Project Concept & Management **Stella Bradley**
Designed by **Paul Montague**

For more books in the series, order online at **herocollector.com**

10 9 8 7 6 5 4 3 2 1
Printed in China.

ISBN 978-1-85875-995-1